Make your speech more impactful

Top 10 tips (+ 1 bonus tip) on making and delivering a great speech

Table of Contents

Introduction

Hi everyone!

Thanks for purchasing this book. I am writing this checklist because I thought it would be helpful for those that are not experienced in public speaking, to understand what elements of a speech will deliver the most impact. The number one thing, no doubt, has to be the content of the speech. You can take a speech with mediocre content, deliver it well and make it a pretty good speech but you will not be able to make it a great speech (i.e., one that has an impact on the audience) without good content. It is the combination of both good content and a refined delivery that makes a speech impactful and this checklist is about the elements of delivery.

I will be talking about ten tips (and a bonus tip) in this checklist:

- Craft an introduction for yourself that gets the audience interested
- Use your speech title in your speech to create a unified message
- Determine the purpose of your speech and make sure your speech fits the purpose
- Memorize your speech
- Use 'precise' language
- Use pauses effectively
- Understand transitions
- Use body language
- Repeat your thesis statement
- Have a strong conclusion
- Relate the speech back to specific members of the audience

Use this handy checklist above of the ten (plus one) tips as you prepare your next speech – each tip will be described in more detail, provide you with a specific example to get you on the right track and have a handy mini checklist that will ensure that your speech is covering the right things to be impactful.

Tip #1 – Craft an introduction for yourself that gets the audience interested

Explanation

All too often, I see speakers who miss the opportunity to connect with the audience even before they come up to speak. The MC or the Host will share the background of the speaker, say the speech title and then welcome the speaker to the stage or lectern. The MC or Host is not thinking about how to make your speech more impactful – that is and should be your responsibility!

The speaker's introduction is a way to bridge the gap between the speaker and the audience. If your goal as a speaker is to reach every single person in the audience, then I think it is safe (and better) to assume that your audience knows nothing about you, nothing about your experience or expertise on the subject and especially nothing about what you will be talking about. Therefore, it is up to you to craft a unique introduction for yourself. A great introduction, I believe, answers three questions:

1. What is your name and speech title

    Who will the audience congratulate and thank after you deliver your speech? All joking aside, your name is a very obvious thing to provide so that you can receive recognition and credit for your speech as well as to build your own personal brand. You will see in the next tip (Tip #2) why providing your speech title can be a great way of making your speech more impactful.

2. What is your experience or expertise on the subject? What makes you qualified to talk about this subject?

    If a lawyer came in to talk about the latest cancer treatments, what would you think about the content of his speech? Even if the content was all true, it would be hard to believe that a lawyer would know so much about medicine or that anyone should believe the lawyer. Whoever asked you to do the speech believes that you are the right person, even if you don't believe in it yourself (although you should!) Provide as much background as you can on your expertise or experience on the speech subject.

    If the subject is on cancer treatments, ask yourself what evidence you can provide that can help give the audience the confidence to believe in your message and the content of your speech. Are you a doctor? Are you an oncologist? How many patients have you treated successfully? Are you the foremost researcher on cancer? A particular type of cancer? Have you written papers? All of the answers to these questions will help provide your introduction and therefore, the speaker (yourself) credibility!

3. Why is this subject relevant to the audience? More specifically, why is THIS subject relevant to THIS audience?

    The first two questions introduce you, your speech title and why you might be a credible speaker, but if the audience does not understand why you are talking to them about this subject, your message will not get through to them.

If an oncologist, who is the foremost expert on cancer treatments, talks to an audience of pilots, what takeaways will the audience get from the oncologist? It is a good idea to address this through the speech introduction so that the audience can at least start to understand why you are speaking to them. One problem that I see speakers make is they go over the time limit because they explain a lot of things that could have been shared in your introduction. Explaining why this speech might be valuable to the audience may be a part of your speech, but that can be done with the speech introduction (or enhanced with the introduction) and therefore, give you more time for your speech.

Example

Let us suppose that I am asked at a leadership conference to deliver a speech on how to speak effectively. Here is an introduction that I would use (note that my name is provided at the end to provide a small amount of 'suspense'):

"Our speaker has been a Toastmaster for seven years, has won multiple speech contests and has had the honour of speaking at Pecha Kucha. He recently served as a Division Governor where he was responsible for seven areas and over forty clubs in the Edmonton area. Our speaker works as a Management Consultant at Deloitte, where he works on honing his communication for clients through oral presentations and written reports.

Our speaker understands that one of the keys to being an effective leader is through clear communication. In his speech, he will cover ten ways to speak effectively and to enhance your leadership skills. These ten ways will cover relevant topics such as learning how to delegate effectively, understanding how to motivate your team and giving and receiving honest feedback from your team. Please help give a warm welcome to our speaker with a speech titled "Becoming a more effective leader through communication", Wang Yip."

Notice in the introduction that I provide my name and speech title, I talk about my credentials as a speaker and as a leader and I talk about some topics in my speech that are relevant to this particular audience attending the leadership conference. I do not provide all the topics in my speech in my introduction – I only provide a few as a way to tease the audience as to what's to come. You might choose not to introduce any topics at all and that is perfectly okay as well; just make sure that the audience gets the answer to the three questions listed above.

Mini checklist - Preparing your introduction

* Does it have a speech title and your name? Your name should be at the end of the introduction to create some 'suspense' even if it is obvious who the speaker is.

* Does it contain your experience or expertise on the subject? What will make you credible as a speaker?

* Does it explain why this subject is relevant to this audience? Why should the audience be listening to you on this subject? Can you make it relevant to their lives in some way?

* Could you add a small teaser to get the audience engaged? Sometimes a relevant teaser can help to get the audience interested in what you have to say.
* Is it short and to the point? It should not be longer than the speech. It should provide enough content to get the audience interested but not give away the whole speech. If the speech introduction is too long, the audience will start to lose interest.

* Does it contain any words or phrases that may be hard to pronounce? Check with the person doing the introduction and make sure that they read it correctly. Also, some MC's / Hosts will ad-lib your introduction – if you do not want this to happen, make sure you tell them to read it word for word specifically.

Tip #2 – Use your speech title in your speech to create a unified message

Explanation

I use this technique all the time whenever I create speeches. The way I go about it is by determining what my speech title is, then writing the whole speech and then figuring out ways to incorporate it inside of my speech.

I like to incorporate my speech title in my speech for a variety of reasons:

- The speech title is one of the first things that the audience hears and it may even be the only thing that they remember. If the speech title is used throughout your speech, it will help to make the speech more memorable because the audience can 'link' different parts of your speech up with your speech title.
- The speech title is used during the speaker introduction and is therefore, the first 'glance' into your speech. Peppering your speech title throughout your speech, and especially at the end of your speech will help to sandwich your speech between the speech titles and provide a more unified and cohesive message. Note: Those were non-intentional puns.
- Every speech has a speech title – why not use it to your advantage to form part of your speech's message?

Example

I once did a speech called "It's never too late" – it's a speech where it is never too late to make a different choice in life. Below, you will find how I used the speech title to my advantage throughout my speech – these are the actual words that I used in my speech:

- At the end of my introduction:
    - [...] this speech is about how it is never too late. Never too late to pursue your life's passion, to reconnect with an old friend or to tell someone that you love them.
- At the end of my first speaking point in my speech body:
    - It is never too late to pursue your life's passion.
- At the end of my second speaking point in my speech body:
    - It is never too late to reconnect with an old friend.
- At the end of my third speaking point in my speech body:
    - It is never too late to tell someone that you love them, even if they have already passed away.
- And finally at the end of my conclusion:
    - Maybe you have found yourself wondering if things would have been different if you had did this or that and now you are trying to figure out if it is too late. Here is your answer, it is never too late to do the things that matter to you.

You can probably imagine that as an audience member, the message that you received was "it is never too late" and each member of the audience got to pick and choose the message that they want imprinted into their minds through each of the scenarios that I took them through.

Mini checklist - Crafting a speech title

* Can your speech title be crafted in a way that can have more than one meaning? Example: I love U2 (the band) OR I love you too – imagine a speech where you saw U2 and Bono comes up to tell you that he loves you.

* Do you use your speech title in the introduction? Do not just put it into the introduction and think that that is okay; try to expand upon it in a meaningful way.

* Do you use your speech title in your body? I like using it as a way to end my speaking points but you can use it as a way to begin them as well.

* Do you use your speech title in your conclusion? Can your speech title be used in your conclusion with a different meaning to enhance your overall message?
* Do you use the speech titles in an effective manner? Does it sound contrived? If so, this might not be the most effective way of using a speech title.

Tip #3 – Determine the purpose of your speech and make sure your speech fits the purpose

Explanation and Examples

Every speech has a purpose and I believe that a speaker cannot write and deliver a great speech without understanding the purpose of their speech and making sure that everything said in their speech supports that purpose. A speech may have multiple general and specific purposes, but the purpose is the first thing that the speaker should determine before writing their speech. Every speech can be categorised in one or more of the four general purposes:

1. Entertain

    A speech that entertains is not necessarily a humorous speech; a speech can be entertaining without getting any laughs at all from the audience but often times, an entertaining speech will get a laugh or two. A speech about the time you mistook a stranger for a friend can be equally entertaining as a speech about the time you were almost mugged while traveling abroad.

    Examples include:
    *   My worst first date
    *   How I almost got mugged in China
    *   My rollercoaster life

    I suppose it helps to think of Entertain and Humorous as part of a Venn diagram. All humorous speeches, I think, are entertaining but not all entertaining speeches are humorous (though I'm sure a large portion of the speeches are).

2. Motivate

A speech that motivates is similar to a speech that persuades, however it is in a different category because it is a speech that inspires the audience members to achieve a higher purpose in life. It is also different because it more often relies on the emotional appeal of the audience member whereas a persuasive speech more often relies on the logical appeal of the audience member.
Examples include:

*   Becoming the leader that you were meant to be
*   Anybody can become an artist
*   Finding your inner child

3. Persuade

A speech that persuades is trying to convince people to change the way they think, the way they might do something or to start doing something that they are not doing.
Examples include:

*   Why you should vote in this upcoming election
*   Apple vs. Android
*   Nuclear power is the power of the future

4. Inform

A speech that informs is any speech that provides useful information to the audience.

Examples include:

*   How to cut a pineapple
*   Understanding black holes
*   Economics 101

Once you have determined the major purpose, you can now start to understand the specific purpose of your speech. The examples listed underneath each major purpose above are examples of the specific purpose of a speech (e.g., a speech that informs provides useful information to the audience but it is specifically a speech about how to cut a pineapple).

Mini checklist - Determining the purpose of your speech

* **Does your speech have a major purpose or purposes?** Is it to inform, entertain, motivate or persuade the audience?

* **Have you determined the specific purpose of your speech?** If yes, what is it?

* **Are you having a hard time determining the purpose of your speech?** If you are having a hard time determining the purpose of your speech, try to think about what state of mind your audience is in before your speech and what you would like them to be in at the end of your speech. (e.g., change in mindset means persuasive or motivate; have a laugh means entertain, etc.)

* **Does each section of your speech support your general and specific purpose?** Read each section of your speech separately and see if it supports your purpose.

* **Does everything in your speech relate back to both your general and specific purpose?** Read the speech from an overall perspective - (i.e., if you are arguing, does one statement logically progress to the next statement; if you are informing the audience on how to cut a pineapple, are the steps chronological?)

Tip #4 – Memorize your speech

Explanation

Let me first say that there is absolutely nothing wrong with reading off of a script – great speeches can be read off of a script; however, even great speeches that are read off of a script are memorized in some part with the script being used as notes to jog the speaker's memory at specific pre-determined times.
I believe that if you can memorize your speech, it is one less thing that will be on your mind when you go up to deliver your speech and the less things that you have to worry about during your speech, the more confident and focused you will be.
Another reason for memorizing your speech instead of reading off a script is that you can maintain your focus on the audience. If you read off a script, every time you look down at your notes is a missed opportunity to maintain eye contact with the audience. How does it feel when someone you are talking to is looking at any place except your face? It feels like they do not care and it feels as if they are just saying anything to get out of talking to you. You may not be able to look into every audience member's face, but memorizing your speech will give you every opportunity to connect to the audience.

Here is a tip for eye contact: some people may find it extremely intense to stare into a person's eyes; try staring at their mouth instead.

Example

How do you memorize a speech – especially huge speeches that take 10, 20, even 30 minutes? Start simple before progressing on to memorizing longer speeches. My strategy for memorizing speeches is comprised of three ideas:

1. Break down the speech into 5 components

The components are as follows: An introduction, three speaking points in the body of your speech and lastly, the conclusion. After creating your speech, take a look at each of the components and determine what general messages you want to pass along to your audience (hint: think about your purpose and how it relates to your speech's purpose). When I craft a speech, I use the rule of threes – my intro will have three speaking points and then a thesis statement (a.k.a. what I am going to talk about in my speech).

The body of the speech will have three speaking points and in each speaking point, there will be three supporting facts (i.e., a total of nine facts for the three speaking points). Finally, the conclusion will summarize the three speaking points and end with my speech title, a relevant quote or a call to action. If you can break down your speech in this way, it will become a lot more manageable than trying to memorize a speech of 500 words.

2. Do not worry too much about the exact wording of the speech

When I first started doing speeches, I thought that the best way to deliver speeches was to memorize the speech word for word. This worked for me, for some time, however, during one of my speeches, I completely forgot what came next and because I was so caught up in delivering my speech word for word, I could not get back on track and had to fumble my way to the end.

If you break down your speech into different components and general ideas, you can go into your speech without having the exact wording in mind and deliver the speech in your own words. In order to deliver your speech in your own words and ensure that you deliver your speech in the time limit set out, you will need to practice your speech before you give it.

3. Practice your speech as much as you can until you get the general ideas right

That takes me to the third idea. It is likely that when you practice the first time using this method, it will be absolutely awful and that is okay. Just like public speaking, the more you practice, the more your speech will improve through your own personal standards of perfection. The first time you go through your speech, do not worry too much if you mess up the wording or go over the time limit. All of these things can be tweaked and improved.

A strange thing will happen when you practice your speech aloud – you will hear things in your speech that sounded okay when you wrote it but now sounds awkward when you say it out loud. Take note of these areas and after going through your speech, tweak those areas of your speech and practice out loud again. Through this process, you will have a good understanding of your speech and be able to handle any wrenches that might be thrown your way.

As an example, if your speech was cut down from 10 minutes to 5 minutes and you memorized your speech word for word, you would not be able to easily cut out half of the words to cut down half of the speech. On the other hand, if you memorized general concepts, it might make sense to only cover two speaking points and shorten your introduction and conclusion to reduce the length of your speech while still delivering the same core message.

Dale Carnegie once said that there are always three speeches for every one you actually gave. The one you practiced, the one you gave, and the one you wish you gave. The more you practice your speech, the closer the speech you gave will be to the one you wish you gave.

Mini checklist - Memorizing your speech

* Have you broken down your speech into smaller, easy-to-memorize components? Is the speech comprised of five general ideas?

* Have you practiced your speech until you feel that you can rearrange or add things into your speech easily without putting in effort to memorize your speech again? A great speaker can shorten or lengthen their speech to react to the audience's needs.

* Are you worried that you will forget your speech? If you are still worried about forgetting your speech, create flash cards with the 5 big ideas in your speech and refer to your flash cards briefly during your speech when needed. This is much less distracting than holding a sheet of notes in your hands in front of you.
* Do you have any quotes or facts that you absolutely need to memorize? If you have any quotes or specific facts that you need to get perfect, spend extra time memorizing them or write them down on the index cards. If you write them down on the index cards, use this wording to tone down the fact that you are reading off of the cue cards: "I have a quote now that I'd like to share with you but I want to get the wording just right", then look down at your cue cards and read it off, trying to maintain as much eye contact as you can with the audience. The same phrase can be used when you have lost your place in a speech and have your notes at the lectern or somewhere convenient.

Tip #5 – Use 'precise' language

Explanation and Examples

We all know people who use big words to sound smart. That is not to say that having a diverse and large vocabulary is not a good thing; however, when you are trying to get your audience to embrace your message through your speech, you have to use language that is simple and easy to understand.

Every speaker and speech has a general and specific purpose and achieving that purpose is easier when you, as the speaker, make it as easy as possible for the audience to understand everything about your speech. Therefore, it is important to use language that is 'precise' and by 'precise', I mean language that is suited and adapted to your audience.

Using precise language means a few things:

- Using simple words instead of large words (i.e., use 'understand' instead of 'comprehend', use 'building' instead of 'constructing')

- Being careful about your use of acronyms – not everyone understands what ROI or NBA are

- Being careful about using jargon or words that are specific to your industry, work, hobby, etc. As an example, a concept like calculus might mean math in university or it might mean the tartar that builds up in your teeth. If you are not sure about the words used in your speech, test it out on your parents or friends and make sure that they are not confused about the meaning of specific words in your speech.

- Understanding the background and culture of your audience – do not assume that everyone in the audience knows what Sesame Street is. If you are not sure if everyone understands, ask the audience but then explain it anyway just in case.

Mini checklist - Using precise language

* Do you use big words when smaller and simpler words would suffice? Do not risk confusing your audience with big words; use simple words that everyone can understand.

* Do you use any acronyms or abbreviations in your speech that others would not understand? Defining the acronyms or abbreviations at the start before using them throughout your speech will help to ensure that everyone knows what you mean when you say "ROI" or "NBA"

* Do you use words that are specific to your industry, hobby, etc.? Try to replace them with words or phrases that have universal meaning.
* Are there noun clusters in your speech? Are there multiple nouns stuck together that can be simplified, e.g., using challenges instead of project outcome setbacks.

* Are you using complicated examples? Try to think of analogies or simpler examples when explaining complex concepts. Think of what your audience would understand and frame it around their experience (e.g., if you have an audience full of doctors, can you explain the concept of bitcoin in terms of medicine or biology?)

Tip #6 – Use pauses effectively

Explanation

Have you ever had a conversation where someone paused in the middle of the conversation and you knew that they were going to say something important? There is something about silence or a pause in a noisy world that captures your attention. Pauses can be used in two different ways:

- Before something important you have to say

- After something important you just said

The next time you have something important to say like a significant quote, a punch line to a joke, or the crux of your speech, take a few seconds before delivering it and then wait a few seconds after. Generally, the pause before is longer than the pause after, but the pause after can give a few seconds to help the audience absorb what you have just said.

Example

I once did a speech entitled "Pause... for effect" which explored the use of pauses in a humorous way. As part of the speech, I listed out all the ways that you could use pauses to enhance the effects of your speech:

- Pausing after asking a question to receive a response or after asking a rhetorical question to let the audience think about the question

- Pausing before a punch line to increase the effect of the joke

- Pausing for dramatic effect, as in pausing before reaching the ultimate climax of a story

- Pausing to transition between topics (this, in combination with the next tip on transition sentences will help you switch topics effectively)

- Pausing after saying something important so that you can gauge how the audience feels and let them 'feel' how important what you just said is

- Pausing after explaining something incredibly complex. Look at the audience and if you see some confused looks, that is your cue to try to explain the concept again but in a different way.

Experiment with the length of the pause – if you are doing a humorous speech, try increasing the amount of time before punch lines (e.g., try counting to 3 before your first punch line, counting to 4 before your second punch line and finally, 5 before your third punch line). It will feel like an extremely long time and it will also feel uncomfortable (which is why you want to experiment with the length of the pause) but it will work and it will have an incredible effect on the audience.

Mini checklist - Using pauses effectively

* Is your speech humorous? Try pausing before your punch line to get more laughs and pausing after to give the audience a chance to laugh – if there are no laughs, make it seem as if you planned it that way and move on.

* Does your speech have quotes? Try pausing before your quote and your audience will know that it is important.

* Does your speech contain a story with a climax? Try pausing from time to time, and especially before your climax to build up the drama and thrill of the story.

* Do you need a way to transition between topics? A pause can help with the transition.

* **Do you explain a difficult concept in your speech?** Using a pause can help you gauge whether your audience understood the concept or whether you need to explain it in a different way.

* **If you are going to use a pause, do you know how long you want to pause?** Try counting to 3 in your head when you want to pause or another number – this can help you make your pauses consistent but also understand what length of pause is optimal for you or your speech.

Tip #7 – Understand transitions

Explanation

Speakers can often underestimate the importance of transitions in their speech. Transitions can help a speaker in a variety of ways:

- It can help bridge two topics to help the audience make the leap of understanding from one topic to the other ·
- It can help to prepare the audience for the next topic; it signals the end of a topic and the start of the next topic
- It can help the audience understand how different topics might relate or not relate to each other

If you have ever had conversations where the conversation made a left turn at some point (a segue way) and there was no context for the turn, you will understand why transitions are important.

Example

There are a number of transitions that I have used in my speeches in order to achieve the goals listed above:

- Using transition words can help with the transitions (examples include: however, but, consequently, although, in contrast).
- If you are explaining a process or making a logical argument, it helps to use words to structure your argument: first, this is the background, second, this is my hypothesis, third, this is the evidence I am using to support my hypothesis.
- There are also a variety of transition phrases that you can use to aid your transition (e.g., ... "that leads me to", "let me now end by"..., "there are a number of reasons

why this is the case", "think back to the situation I explained at the beginning of my speech", "what I explained shows"...)

Mini checklist - Understanding transitions

* Do you understand what kind of transitions you need from the type of speech you have? If you have a persuasive speech, you will want to lay out the facts and evidence in a logical manner.

* Do you use transitions whenever there is a change in topic in your speech? Consider if you need transitions or not – some transitions may not need a specific transition sentence.

* Can you use transitions in your speech to help the audience understand leaps in your speech? If you make a leap in logic, even if it is a small leap, it will always help when you use transition words that can help your audience understand how you got from one point to the next.
* Are you using appropriate transition words that help your audience see your argument or story the way you see it? Does the next point follow from the first point? Use phrases like 'consequently', or 'it follows that'.

* Does the next point not follow from the first point? Use phrases like 'in contrast' or 'let's consider something else'

Tip #8 – Use body language

Explanation

Everyone knows how important body language is to the speech; in fact, there is an oft-quoted figure of how communication is 70 percent body language (the figure is higher or lower depending on the sources you look at). Nonetheless, body language is extremely important; used in the right way, it can enhance the message of your speech.
You might be surprised but body language can be many different things and not just how your body moves. It can also include:

- Your facial gestures (smiling, frowning, raised eyebrows, holding your nose, etc.)
- Everything about your body, either dynamic (moving) or static (not moving), this can include:
  - Head – shaking your head, turning your head from side to side, looking up, looking down
  - Shoulders – shrugging your shoulders, slumped shoulders
  - Chest – breathing in and out, sucked in
  - Arms and hands – moving, pointing, gesturing, waving
  - Hips – hula hooping, hip checking
  - Legs – kicking, dancing, walking

All of these 'movements' can help to emphasize a certain point in your speech and enhance the overall message of your speech.

Example

I want you to imagine for a second that your boss is telling you that you need to improve your sales and he has different looks on his face:

- A surprised look – perhaps he is shocked that you, a top salesman, is not selling as much as he expected
- A smile or a pleased look – he is absolutely pleased with the sales that you are generating and is cheekily telling you to improve your sales
- A frown – he is not happy with the sales you are generating
- Tears in his eyes – his business is going under because of the lack of sales you have
- A confused look – the sales you are generating did not match his expectations

You can start to see now that even though the words stay the same, the body language that you portray to the person or audience you are talking to can change or enhance your message. If your body language is not delivering the same type of message as the words you are saying, the audience will be confused over what type of message you are trying to pass to them and as a result, may not get the message you intended.

Here is one way I like to use body language that is not dependent on the message of your speech. For every speech that I create that has an introduction, three speaking points in the body and a conclusion, I will transition in the following way: when I want to transition topics, I pause, walk from one side of the room to the other and then begin my next topic. It is a simple and effective way of letting the audience know that you are done with the topic and that you will start a new topic.

Another way that I like to emphasize different points is through movement while talking and building up to an important quote or climax. While talking and building up to the climax, I will step forward, pause and then say something that the audience knows is important. If I have successively important things to say, I might take a step forward for every important thing I have to say with the climax stepping forward and getting as close to the audience as I can possibly get.

Note that body language can be so much more than just moving around the room, it can be your hand gestures, it can be your facial gestures, it can be your shoulders, hips, legs or if you are like me, it can be your big fat behind ;) Don't be afraid to experiment with different ways to move around and combine it with the words in your speech!

Mini checklist - Using body language

* Are you aware of the body language you are using in your speech? Try rehearsing in front of the mirror to see what type of body language you naturally exhibit.

* Do you see what kind of natural body language you already exhibit? Once you are aware of the body language you naturally have, determine what seems comfortable to you and try to use it to your advantage.

* Do you want to naturally transition from one topic to another? Try moving from one side of the room to another when transitioning from one topic to the next topic.

* Do you want to emphasize an important quote, statistic or statement? Try stepping forward, pausing and then delivering it.
* Do you want to emphasize successive important points? Try stepping forward with each important point.

* Do you want to emphasize how bad of an idea something is?
Try stepping back and throwing your hands up when talking about a bad idea.

Tip #9 – Use your thesis statement effectively

Explanation

First, what is the thesis statement? For essay writers, the thesis statement is the statement in your introduction that introduces the point that you will prove in the body of your speech. For speakers, it is the three (or however many you have covered in your speech) speaking points that you will be discussing in your speech.
The aim of this tip is to make it as easy as possible for the audience to understand your speech. Remember, it is the speaker's responsibility to make it easy for the audience to understand the speech and that means breaking down the points into digestible, easy-to-remember statements. If the audience can follow and understand your speech then it increases the chances that your audience will absorb the message you are delivering.

Here are a few sample thesis statements to help you understand what they are for speeches:

- "In this speech, I will be discussing why the city should invest in public transit through addressing three questions: how public transit will help reduce congestion, how public transit will help reduce pollution and how public transit will increase our overall standard of life"
- In the next few minutes, I will share with you how I became a business owner, first, I learned about what a business was, second, I failed a lot, lastly I persevered and finally found my passion

Example

Ever since someone taught me this technique to repeat my thesis statement throughout my speech, I have used it for all of my speeches to great effect.

"Tell them what you're going to talk about, talk about it, and then tell them what you told them"

As an example, I will use this structure for a speech:

> Introduction
>
> At the end of the introduction – "I am going to tell you about three things that will make your speech impactful: body language, transitions and pauses"
>
> First speaking point on body language – "First, I will talk about body language."
>
> ...
>
> Second speaking point on transitions – "Second, I will talk about transitions"
>
> ....
>
> Third speaking point on pauses – "Lastly, I will talk about pauses"
>
> ....
>
> Conclusion – "I just told you about the three things that will make your speech impactful – body language, transitions and pauses."

Notice how I used the formula to tell them what I am going to talk about in the speech, talk about it and then tell them what I just told them. As a speaker, it seems like your speech is logical and organized but that is partly because you have been immersed in your speech for days (or weeks). As an audience member for many speeches, the structure makes it easy for me to follow, understand and remember.

Mini checklist - Using your thesis statement effectively

* Do you have a thesis statement in your speech? Does the audience know what you will be sharing in your speech?

* Do you repeat the thesis statement throughout your speech? Is it in your introduction, your speaking points and your conclusion?

* Is it easy for the audience to follow along? If you stopped at any point in your speech, would they be able to tell you where you are in your speech or what you are talking about? Whenever you pause, look to the audience and see if there are confused looks on their faces. They might not be following your speech and this may be a cue to either backtrack in your speech or to explain what you are talking about and how it relates to your speech.

Tip #10 – Have a strong conclusion

Explanation

Typically, the audience will only remember a few things about your speech (hey, they cannot help it! They have a limited memory and can only hold a few things in their short term memory). A case can be made then for ending your speech on a strong note as that is typically what the audience will remember about your speech. If you leave them with a strong impression of your speech in the end, they may feel strongly about your speech overall because the last thing that you left the audience with is something impactful.

Example

A strong conclusion can help to build the case for the overall message of your speech. A speech that begins strong, has strong, logical arguments to convince the audience of something and then a weak conclusion may not convince the audience of anything at all. I believe that strong conclusions are not just summaries or recaps of what you just talked about in your speech; a strong conclusion will 'proceed' to the next step.

What I mean with proceeding to the next step is that if it is a speech on a research topic, it will recap but then talk about where the research might go next or what this research might be the foundation of next. If it is a speech that entertains, it might end on a funny anecdote (even if the funniest joke was used for the climax). If it is a speech about persuasion or motivation, it will talk about something the audience can do in the next hour or day that can make a difference.

In other words, it is not just a straight recap of what you talked about in your speech but builds upon the message in a meaningful way.

There are a few ways to end your speeches or craft a strong conclusion. Some of these ways include:

- If persuading, recapping your three points and then coming to a logical conclusion
- If motivating or inspiring your audience, providing them with a call to action (i.e., now that you know the benefits of walking every day, I encourage you to spend a few minutes walking, even if it's just around the block)
- If entertaining, conclude your speech with a punch line to a joke or a surprise twist
- If informing, conclude your speech with a surprising fact or how it is relevant to the audience

One of my speeches was about the Drake Equation. For those of you that do not know what it is, the Drake Equation is an equation that estimates the number of active and communicative extraterrestrial life in the universe based on a number of different factors. It first multiplies the estimated number of civilizations in the galaxy that would have communication technology. It then multiplies this with the average rate of star formation in the galaxy. It then multiples this with the fraction of stars that would have planets revolving around it. And on and on with a variety of factors multiplied until we reach a number at the end that tells us how many civilizations Earth could communicate with. My purpose for this speech was to inform, but for my conclusion, I used the Drake Equation to estimate the number of girls that were in Edmonton that were single and that could be potential dating partners. It was an interesting twist in my speech and one that I do not think that my audience saw coming, which made it even more effective and humorous in the end. This is one of my favourite ways of ending speeches (i.e., a surprise twist at the end) and it requires some careful thought and planning but when it works, it can be incredibly effective. The audience may not remember the exact formula for the Drake Equation but they can certainly explain the general concept around the equation through the humorous example I provided in my speech.

Mini checklist - Having a strong conclusion

* **What is the purpose of your speech? How can you create a conclusion that will meet the purpose of your speech while leaving a strong impression in the audience's minds?** Understand the purpose of your speech and make sure that your conclusion fits with that purpose.

* **Is your speech persuasive?** Try recapping your points and then coming to a logical conclusion OR try addressing some of the audience's likely objections to the evidence that you have presented.

* **Is your speech to inform?** Try creating a surprise twist with the information that you have just shared. If the twist is not right for your type of speech, try presenting the strong facts or leaving the audience with a yearning to learn more about the subject, e.g., leave them with a mystery

* **Is your speech to motivate or inspire?** Remind them of why it is so important to become better and provide them with a small but tangible action item that they can do to improve their lives.

* **Is your speech to entertain?** End with a strong joke or a surprising twist to the story.

Bonus tip – Relate the speech back to specific members of the audience

Imagine that a speaker is on the stage and they mention your name during the speech! How would it make you feel? How would it make the audience feel?

I have done this on occasion – when I talk to members of the audience and have shared stories with them, I can sometimes relate the audience members or their stories back to my speech and I will point this out.

Although I suppose it can be embarrassing for that audience member, it can also be an incredibly effective way of connecting to your audience and a subtle way of showing that you are a confident speaker (good speakers can incorporate new information into their speech on the fly; they could not have prepared that in advance if they just met the audience member moments before the speech).

In order to connect to specific audience members, you will have to mingle or network before your speech. Try to connect to one or two people and ask them what brought them to the conference or event.

Try to listen and understand exactly why they are there. Also, make sure that you know their names very well; you would not want to mispronounce a person's name or say the wrong name during your speech. As you are the expert on your own speech, try to figure out ways to incorporate what you have heard into your speech (the introduction would be a natural way to do this as that is where you would normally tell the audience how your speech will address their concerns).

The next time you deliver a speech, think about how you can incorporate audience members and their needs or desires into your speech and see how impactful your speech can become.

Thank you!

If you have made it this far, I wanted to thank you for reading. My sole purpose is to provide the tips I have learned over the years to as many people as I know so that they can learn what I have learned.

That being said, I have a favour to ask of you. I am extremely interested in hearing what you thought about the list and have a few questions that I would like you to think about and answer for me if you can. Feel free to pick and choose the questions you want to answer.

- Did any of the tips surprise you? Which tip?
- Which one of the tips did you find the most useful? Why?
- Which one of the tips did you find the least useful? Why?
- What one tip / example / explanation will you take away and use for your next speech?
- What, if anything, are you trying to improve about your communication skills?
- Were you looking for anything specific that I did not cover? What was it?
- Any comments about this speech checklist in general?

I would love to hear from you – leave me a review on Amazon! Thanks again for reading and I hope you are able to use these tips for your next speech =)

More Books by Wang

How To Create and Deliver Great Speeches (A Seven Day Approach) – Go from no speech and no experience to writing and delivering a great speech in a week.
100+ Tips For Speakers – 100+ tips for speakers on a range of topics including preparing for a speech, delivering a speech and concluding a speech (and everything in between).

Preview from 100+ Tips for Speakers

Chapter 4: Speech do's and don'ts

"Mistakes are always forgivable, if one has the courage to admit them." - Bruce Lee

After doing over 50 speeches, evaluating over 100 speeches and judging various speech contests, there are a number of speech do's and don'ts that you should be aware of and I share them here:

Speech do's
* **Be social** - Try to talk to other people before your speech, especially people that you might be delivering your speech to. This can help you calm your nerves and it can be quite a confidence boost to see someone in the crowd that you are familiar with. People want you to succeed (and this is especially the case if they have gotten to know you).
* **Talk to the organizer of the event** - It can be a nice way to break the ice and to learn about issues that previous speakers have faced and what the organizer (or you) can do to address them (e.g., a loud air conditioner in the back).

* **Make sure that any visuals you present can be seen by all audience members** - If any visuals cannot be seen by audience members, you might be able to describe the picture but I recommend that you either use visuals that are large enough to be seen by everyone (even those at the very back of the venue) or do not use visuals at all.

* **Ask the organizer for a glass of water** - This isn't needed for all speeches but for especially long speeches, a glass of water can go a long way in parching your throat and giving you a much needed break (imagine talking for hours - I can't imagine doing it without small breaks in between!)

* **Dress appropriately** - If you are not sure of how you should dress for your speech, dress more formally than you think you need to and dress down if appropriate. You can always dress down but you can't always dress more formally if the occasion necessitates it. Depending on the event, it might be more appropriate to dress down to the level of the audience (to signify that you're not different from them) or to dress one level above the audience (e.g., suit if the audience is mostly wearing jeans) to project professionalism.

* **Walk confidently up to the stage** - Everything leading up to your speech (your speech introduction, how you walk up, whether you are smiling as you walk up) helps give the audience the impression that everything will be a success and that they will get a lot out of the speech. Not doing these things may make the audience question you even before you deliver your speech!

www.ingramcontent.com/pod-product-compliance
Lightning Source LLC
Chambersburg PA
CBHW050756290526
45792CB00008B/2200